THE BEST LITTLE
BARBECUE
COOKBOOK

by Karen Adler

CELESTIALARTS
Berkeley, California

Special thanks to
Mary Ann Duckers, Judith Fertig, Cheryl and Bill Jamison,
Janeyce Michel-Cupito, Ann O'Meara, and Karen Putman
for their recipe contributions to this cookbook.
Also, a special thanks to everyone at Ten Speed Press,
especially Dennis Hayes and my editor, Veronica Randall.

CELESTIALARTS

P.O. Box 7123
Berkeley, CA 94707

Printed in Singapore.

Cover design: Catherine Jacobes
Cover art: Paul Keppel
Interior illustrations: Barry's Clip Art, Basting brush by Brad Greene
Text design: Greene Design

Library of Congress Catalog Card Number: 00-131234

Other cookbooks in this series:
Best Little BBQ Sauces Cookbook
Best Little Grilling Cookbook
Best Little Marinades Cookbook

Celestial Arts titles are distributed in Canada by Ten Speed Canada, in the
United Kingdom and Europe by Airlift Books, in South Africa by Real Books,
in Australia by Simon & Schuster Australia, in New Zealand by Southern
Publishers Group, and in Southeast Asia by Berkeley Books.

Introduction

Barbecue, barbeque, bar-b-que, bar-b-q, b-b-q, bb-que, bbq! There are so many different spellings and definitions of barbecue, and to further complicate things, the word "barbecue" can be used as either a noun or a verb depending on what we're doing. For example, we can invite friends over to a backyard barbecue (the noun) and serve anything from hot dogs and baked beans to sesame-crusted catfish, or we can throw some hamburgers on the grill and say we are barbecuing (the verb). The same is true for grilling and smoking. And just when you thought you had this straight in your mind, you can smoke on a grill, you can grill with wood, charcoal, gas, or electricity, or even in your oven or on your stove top!

Thoroughly confused? Don't be. Whether you're cooking with charcoal, gas, or electricity, the recipes in this book are adaptable to just about any method.

It's a marvelous irony that barbecuing has become the trendiest way to cook because it is also the oldest way to cook. I like to picture our ancient ancestors as the original backyard barbecuers, although they most likely grilled in open pits in front of their caves rather than in Weber kettles

on redwood decks out by the pool. And, of course, their menus ran to tenderloin of mastodon and mammoth burgers rather than tenderloin of beef and shish kabob. But the cooking principles are pretty much the same as they probably were thousands of years ago: letting the fire die down to coals produces a piece of meat that is cooked through but not burned (as opposed to throwing it directly into the flames), and covering the whole thing up (as in a lid on your Weber kettle or burial in the ground out in front of the cave) will slow-cook your meat and produce a piece of meat that is tender and has a wonderful smokey flavor. No doubt, a daring cave cook tried throwing some aromatic herbs onto the coals and noticed how the flavor of the meat was affected, and I can just picture someone spilling some honey on a piece of grilling meat, and thus the first glaze was created.

Barbecue Basics

Grills and smokers are available in a variety of sizes, prices, and fuel choices: gas, electric, pellet, and charcoal/hardwood. Gas and electric grills are quick to start and easy to clean. When grilling on a gas or electric grill, *always* follow the manufacturer's directions. Charcoal grills come in all sizes and shapes, from the kettle-shaped patio grill to trailer-sized rigs with hitches. Pellet smokers use compressed wood pellets as fuel and are also easy to clean. Smokers come in a range of sizes from the popular bullet-shaped water-smoker to commercial sized units as big as a semitrailer. Whatever unit you choose, it must have a lid or cover in order to smoke. A water pan is also preferred because it keeps the food moist during the long slow-smoking cooking time. Thermometers that gauge the interior temperature of the smoker are particularly useful because for most smoke recipes a 225 degree F temperature needs to be maintained during the cooking process.

Basically there are two methods of barbecuing: grilling, which is a dry-heat method of cooking either directly or indirectly over red-hot coals, and smoking, which is a method of slow cooking indirectly over a low temperature heat source with wood added for smoke. Temperatures range from about 200 to 250 degrees F. Cooking indirectly means to cook away from the heat rather than grilling directly over the fire or heat source. Gas and electric grills can create smoke by using a wood box containing water-soaked wood chips placed close to the heat source. Or loosely wrap soaked wood chips in an aluminum foil packet with a few holes poked in the top of the packet to release the smoke. (Do not place wood chips or chunks directly on a gas grill because they may clog the burners as they disintegrate.) Place the meat that is to be cooked on the elevated rack as far away from the gas burner or electric coil as possible, close the lid, and maintain a constant temperature of about 225 degrees F.

The charcoal units use hardwood, lump charcoal, or charcoal briquettes with soaked wood chips or chunks added directly to the fire. Starting a charcoal fire is easy with a charcoal chimney. Just put some crumpled paper in the bottom, place 10 to 15 lumps of charcoal in the top of the chimney, and place on top of your grill. Light the paper and the coals will be white hot in about 15 minutes. Place the ashen coals on one side of the grill and a water pan on the other side. Grill over the hot coals to sear and mark your meat. Then move the meat to the indirect side of the grill over the water pan. Add water-soaked wood to the charcoal and close the lid to smoke. The charcoal and wood may have to be replenished several times depending on cooking time. Use a thermometer to gauge your heat.

The bullet-shaped water smoker is one of the most popular smokers for the backyard barbecuer. They come in charcoal, gas, or electric. They are easy to assemble and are reasonably priced.

Follow the manufacturer's instructions for best results. The electric model is very easy to use. Three or four water-soaked wood chunks are placed around the electric coil in the bottom of the smoker. There is a water pan that fits above the heat and there are usually two racks above the water pan for placing as much as a turkey and two roasts. Then close the lid, plug it in, and it begins to smoke. My rule of thumb for most meats is to cook for about 20 to 30 minutes per pound of meat in the smoker. Use a thermometer to test the meat for best results.

Estimating cooking times is the only real challenge, because the time required to cook a meat varies due to the temperature of the fire and the elements of nature outside. (Is it raining, windy, cold, or hot?) Use the suggested cooking times given in each recipe. But a meat thermometer will be your ally with the safe internal meat temperatures printed on the thermometer.

TOOLS FOR BETTER BARBECUING:

◆ A stiff wire brush with a scraper makes cleaning the grill/smoker easy, especially if you tackle this job while the grill is still warm.

◆ Use a natural bristle basting brush to brush oil on the grill grates to prevent food from sticking and get a separate brush for basting foods during cooking.

◆ Heat-resistant mitts offer the best hand protection, especially when you need to touch hot metals during the cooking process.

◆ Long-handled, spring-loaded tongs are easier to use than the scissors type. Unlike a meat fork, tongs won't pierce the meat and allow the delicious juices to escape. They are great for turning chicken pieces, steaks, vegetables, skewers, and the like.

◆ Aluminum pans and foil are useful for removing meats and vegetables onto and off of the barbecue. They make for easy cleanup, too.

◆ Kabob and vegetable baskets are time-savers. Instead of threading cubed foods onto skewers, just cut your food into chunks, drop them into the basket, and you're ready to grill in a snap. And again, no holes to allow juice and flavor to escape. Two-sided fish grilling racks with long handles are also great tools that keep your fish from falling part.

◆ A grill wok and long-handled wooden spoons or tongs for stirring in the wok are newer additions to the grilling tools arsenal.

◆ Apply nonstick cooking spray to the grill grates to help prevent sticking before you light the fire.

◆ Thermometers make guesswork unnecessary. You'll need a grill thermometer to place inside the cooker for gauging the cooker's temperature and a meat thermometer to insert into the meat that you're cooking to check the internal temperature.

WOOD CHIPS:

Different smokey flavors come from adding aromatic woods such as mesquite, hickory, oak, maple, pecan and pecan shells, and alder and fruit woods like cherry, apple, pear, and grapevines to your cooking fire. Soaked woody herb stalks added to the grill fire offer another means of flavor enhancement. The heavenly odor in your backyard and the extra flavor in your foods are your rewards. Hardwoods like mesquite and oak burn hot. Wood chips, shavings, and sawdust are best for quick grilling. All wood should be water-soaked for at least 30 minutes prior to smoking. Keep a plastic container filled with wood chips or chunks in water. Compressed wood pellets or larger chunks of wood are best for slow-smoking. Wood logs are often used in big-rig smokers used by professional cooks, caterers, and barbecue competitors.

STOCKING THE PANTRY:

Keeping your outdoor cook's pantry stocked with your favorite items is a wonderful way to save time and keep you inspired. Your preferences in food will dictate the items you'll keep on hand and, as you experiment with new barbecue recipes and styles, they will change and expand to the more exotic. We start here with the most essential basic pantry items.

Basic seasoning choices: assorted peppers and salts like freshly ground black, red, and white pepper; pepper blends such as lemon pepper or seasoned pepper; sea salt, kosher salt, and flavored salts such as garlic, onion, and celery salt; plus garlic and onion powders. Chilies to stock include chili powder, paprika, red pepper, and red pepper flakes. Brown and white sugar and honey are good sweeteners to always have on hand.

Fresh or dried herbs thrown on a charcoal fire create a heavenly aroma. Just soak either fresh or dried herbs in water and sprinkle onto your charcoal fire. If using a gas grill, wrap the herbs in foil, puncture the foil with several small holes, and place on top of your grill. Keep on hand a selection of your favorites like basil, oregano, parsley, rosemary, tarragon, sage, and thyme. Spices to include are dry mustard, ginger, cinnamon, cloves (whole and ground), coriander, and cumin.

Basic vinegars and oils: distilled white vinegar, cider vinegar, red, white, and rice vinegars, and vegetable, canola, olive, and/or peanut oil.

CONDIMENTS:

Bottled barbecue sauces, mustards, ketchup, soy sauce, Worcestershire, hot sauces, liquors and liqueurs, and fruit juices. Store-bought marinades and grill seasonings, fruit jellies and preserves, chutneys, relishes, and salsas are all convenient options and are available in grocery and gourmet stores. And, of course, keep batches of your own creations on hand. Be creative and try making your own sauces and glazes. You'll be surprised how easy they are to make and how well they keep in airtight containers in your refrigerator.

BARBECUE RECIPES

Charcoal Barbecued Beef Brisket

Barbecued beef brisket is a perennial favorite, especially since it makes such delicious sandwiches anointed with barbecue sauce the next day. If you want to serve this for dinner, start in the morning because this roast will take all day long.

1 (10- to 12-pound) beef brisket roast, trimmed
2 tablespoons olive oil

BRISKET RUB:

1/2 cup paprika
1/4 cup cayenne pepper
1/4 cup granulated garlic
1/4 cup black pepper

WOOD:

4 or 5 chunks each water-soaked hickory and
   cherry wood

Using a brush, paint the brisket roast evenly with the olive oil. Combine the rub ingredients, cover the roast evenly with the rub (using your hands will be the easiest), then set aside to allow it to come to room temperature.

In a smoker, prepare a charcoal fire on one side. Set a water pan on the other side. When the fire is hot, add 2 chunks each of hickory and cherry wood to the charcoal. Bring heat to 225 degrees F, place the brisket over the water pan (indirect heat), cover, and maintain the temperature.

Smoke the brisket for 12 hours, keeping the temperature steady by replenishing the charcoal and wood. Remove the brisket from the smoker, wrap in plastic wrap, then cover completely with aluminum foil. Return the covered brisket to the smoker and cook for another 3 hours.

Remove from the smoker and let stand for 10 minutes. Unwrap, then slice thinly against the grain of the meat and serve with your favorite barbecue sauce.

Serves 8 to 10

Smoked and Peppered Beef Rib Roast

A standing rib roast creates a sumptuous, regal centerpiece for the company dinner table.

1 (4- to 6-pound) standing rib roast
¼ cup olive oil
1 tablespoon granulated garlic
½ cup cracked peppercorns

WOOD:
4 to 5 chunks of water-soaked wood (oak or
    mesquite)

Prepare the grill or smoker to a temperature of between 225 to 250 degrees F.

Rub the roast with olive oil, sprinkle with granulated garlic, and thoroughly coat with pepper. Place roast, fat side up, on a grill rack.

Smoke over an indirect fire for $2^1/4$ to 3 hours, or until meat thermometer inserted in the thickest part of the roast registers 140 degrees F for rare.

Remove from the smoker, wrap tightly in heavy foil, and allow to rest for 15 to 20 minutes. Carve it at the table for the visual delight of your guests, and serve with mashed potatoes and sautéed vegetables.

Serves 8

Slow-Roasted Prime Rib of Beef

Woody stalks of rosemary, lavender, basil, or sage added to a barbecue fire create an incomparable aroma in your backyard.

8 pound rib roast, well trimmed and tied

1 large clove garlic, mashed

1/4 teaspoon salt

1/4 teaspoon freshly ground black pepper

1/4 teaspoon oregano and rosemary

1 onion, peeled and coarsely chopped

2 carrots, peeled and coarsely chopped

2 stalks celery, coarsely chopped

1 cup red wine

1/2 cup water

Dash of Worcestershire sauce

WOOD:

6 to 7 chunks of water-soaked mesquite and
   apple wood

Remove rib roast from the refrigerator to allow it to come to room temperature. Combine the garlic, salt, pepper, oregano, and rosemary and rub seasonings into the roast. Place meat fat side up in a roasting pan.

Prepare a water smoker and add 3 of the water-soaked chunks of wood. Place meat in the smoker and cook for 2 1/2 hours. Open the smoker and scatter the chopped vegetables in the pan around the roast. Add more wood and close the smoker. Cook for about 2 1/2 hours for rare (140 degrees F on a meat thermometer), or longer for well done. Total cooking time should be approximately 30 to 45 minutes per pound.

When done, take roast out of the smoker and place on a carving board. Let rest for about 10 minutes before carving. Place the vegetables in a serving bowl and keep warm.

If there is enough meat juice in the roasting pan, prepare a red wine au jus: Remove excess fat from the pan, place pan over low heat, and scrape loose the pieces of meat and vegetables. Bring heat up to medium-high. Add 1 cup of red wine and 1/2 cup of water to deglaze the pan. Season with salt and pepper and a dash of Worcestershire sauce. Cook for about 2 to 3 minutes to reduce the liquid slightly, strain, and adjust seasonings. Serve warm with the roast beef and vegetables.

Serves 12

Sublime Beef Tenderloin

Beef tenderloin is best rare to medium-rare, so be careful not to overcook it. This recipe is adapted from Cheryl and Bill Jamison's cookbook Sublime Smoke.

1 1/2 pounds beef tenderloin

2 tablespoons Pickapeppa sauce

1 teaspoon garlic salt

1 teaspoon orange zest

1 teaspoon brown sugar

1/2 teaspoon freshly grated ginger

1/2 teaspoon ground allspice

WOOD:

3 to 5 chunks of water-soaked oak and
   apple wood

Place tenderloin in a large, sealable plastic bag. In a small bowl, combine Pickapeppa sauce, garlic salt, orange zest, brown sugar, ginger, and allspice. Pour mixture over tenderloin, seal the bag, and marinate for 1 to 2 hours in the refrigerator. Remove tenderloin from the refrigerator and allow it to come to room temperature (about 1 hour).

In the meantime, prepare a barbecue grill for indirect cooking by building a hot fire on 1 side and placing the water pan on the opposite side. Over the hot fire, sear the meat quickly on all sides. Add 3 wood chunks to the fire. Transfer the tenderloin to the indirect side of the smoker and cook it until the internal temperature reaches 140 degrees F, about 70 to 80 minutes. Midway through the cooking time, check the wood. If it has burned down, add 1 or 2 more chunks.

Take the tenderloin off the grill and tent it with foil to keep it warm. Let rest for 10 minutes, then slice and serve.

Serves 6

Stir-Grilled Beef with Sesame Snow Peas

It is so nice to grill most of your meal, creating minimal mess in the kitchen. Accompany this dish with orange zested rice or prepare extra marinade to toss with cooked noodles for an Asian side dish.

You'll need a grill wok to make this recipe and a couple of extra-long-handled wooden spoons or tongs.

1 pound beef sirloin steak

1 small yellow squash, sliced

1/2 pound snow peas

1 cup fresh bean sprouts

1/2 cup sliced green onions

WOOD:

1 cup of water-soaked mesquite wood chips

SESAME-SOY MARINADE:

1/2 cup soy sauce

2 tablespoons water

1 tablespoon toasted sesame oil

2 cloves garlic, minced

$1/8$ teaspoon red pepper flakes

Trim fat from beef and slice into $1/8$-inch-thick strips. Place beef, squash, snow peas, bean sprouts, and green onions in a bowl. Combine marinade ingredients and pour over beef mixture. Refrigerate for 15 to 30 minutes.

Prepare a hot fire and add the water-soaked wood chips to the fire.

Pour beef mixture into a greased grill wok over the sink and drain liquid. Place a pan under the wok and carry out to the grill. Stir-grill for 6 to 8 minutes using long-handled wooden spoons or long tongs to toss the mixture several times during grilling. Move grill wok to indirect side of grill and cover grill with lid. Continue cooking for an additional 3 to 4 minutes to heat thoroughly.

Serves 4

Kansas City Strip Steaks with Grilled Red Peppers and Onions

This is a beautiful and easy dinner to prepare in less than 30 minutes. Stretch your dollar by slicing steaks into strips to serve 4.

1 clove garlic, minced

2 tablespoons dried basil

2 tablespoons dried oregano

1 teaspoon freshly ground black and red pepper

2 Kansas City strip steaks, 8 to 10 ounces each

2 tablespoons olive oil

2 tablespoons red wine vinegar

2 red bell peppers, seeded and sliced

1 large red onion, sliced

1/4 cup Romano cheese, for garnish

WOOD:

About 1 cup of water-soaked maple and
    cherry chips

In a small bowl, combine garlic, basil, oregano, and pepper. Rub each steak with 1 tablespoon of the seasoning. In a separate small bowl, whisk together the oil and vinegar and then add to the remaining seasoning. Whisk to combine and set aside.

Prepare a medium-hot fire. Place vegetables in a grill wok and steaks on the barbecue rack over the coals. Grill steaks for 15 minutes for medium doneness. Grill vegetables for about 12 to 15 minutes, turning several times and spooning with herb-oil mixture while cooking. Transfer vegetables to a bowl and toss with the Romano cheese. Serve alongside the steaks.

Serves 2

Sirloin Steak in Kabob Baskets

Kabob baskets are a great addition to your gadget cache. They are an alternative time-saver to skewering and because they don't pierce the meat, no juices can escape during cooking.

1 pound beef sirloin steak

1 zucchini

1 8-ounce carton of button mushrooms

2 ears fresh sweet corn

1 red onion

1/2 cup Italian salad dressing

WOOD:

1 cup of water-soaked pecan wood chips or
   shells

 Trim steak and cut into 1-inch cubes. Cut squash into 1-inch-thick slices. Cut corn into 8 pieces. Cut onion into 8 wedges. Combine meat, vegetables, and Italian dressing in a large sealable plastic bag. Marinate in the refrigerator for at least 1 hour or overnight.

Prepare a hot fire. Place a combination of ingredients in 4 kabob baskets. Add pecan chips to the hot fire and grill kabobs for 6 to 8 minutes until corn is tender and beef is medium-rare to medium.

Serves 4

Honey-Mustard Glazed Pork Roast

A succulent glazed pork roast with the subtly sweet flavor of honey and orange zest is perfect for company.

1 (3½- to 4-pound) pork roast

1 cup of wildflower honey

1 cup of zesty barbecue sauce

2 tablespoons fresh orange zest

¼ cup fresh orange juice

¼ cup country-style German mustard

1 tablespoon Worcestershire sauce

1 teaspoon grated fresh ginger

½ teaspoon salt

¼ teaspoon ground red pepper

WOOD:

5 to 6 chunks of water-soaked apple and
   hickory wood

Prepare smoker for 225 degree F indirect cooking. Place 3 water-soaked apple and hickory wood chunks over the charcoal.

In a small bowl, combine all the ingredients except the pork and set aside. Place pork roast fat-side up in smoker and smoke for 45 minutes. Turn the roast, brush it with the glaze, and cook for 3 to 4 more hours, basting every 20 minutes. Add additional wood after about 2 hours. Keep smoking and basting until the roast is done (when a meat thermometer inserted in the thickest part of the roast registers 160 to 165 degrees F). Remove roast from the grill, cover with plastic wrap, and let stand for 10 minutes before slicing and serving.

Serves 8

Kansas City-Style Barbecued Ribs

The flavor of celery seed adds a delicious dimension to these sassy and spicy ribs. Serve on a platter with plain white sandwich bread with dill pickle slices and extra sauce on the side. These ribs also good the next day served cold.

3 whole slabs of loin baby back pork ribs
   (about 4 pounds)

4 tablespoons sugar

2 tablespoons garlic salt

2 tablespoons ground black pepper

2 tablespoons paprika

2 tablespoons celery seed

1 (12-ounce) can of beer

1 bottle of spicy tomato barbecue sauce

WOOD:

5 to 6 chunks of water-soaked wood (apple,
   oak, or cherry)

The day before cooking, use needle nose pliers to grab the membrane on the underside of each slab of ribs, and pull off in one motion. Combine the dry ingredients and rub over the entire surface of the meat. Cover with plastic wrap and let the flavors blend overnight in the refrigerator.

In a smoker, build an indirect charcoal fire with a water pan on the other side. When the fire is hot, add about 3 chunks of wood. Maintain a 225 degree F temperature. Place the ribs in the cooker on a rack above the water pan and smoke for around 2 hours, or until the meat pulls back from the bone about $1/2$ inch. Check the wood; if it has burned down, add additional chunks now. Turn the ribs over, baste with the beer, and cook for 1 hour longer, basting every 10 to 15 minutes. The more moisture, the better the ribs. Finally, baste the ribs with a spicy barbecue sauce for the last 30 minutes of cooking.

Serves 6

Glazed Ham with Red Currant Fruit Compote

Serve this ham for a spring or summer feast accompanied by fresh garden green beans or asparagus and the Red Currant Fruit Compote.

1 (5- to 7-pound) bone-in ham (shank or butt)

20 cloves

2 cups red currant preserves

2 tablespoons cider vinegar

2 teaspoons dry mustard

WOOD:

5 to 6 chunks of water-soaked wood (apple, oak, or cherry)

RED CURRANT FRUIT COMPOTE:

2 cups bite-size chunks ripe honeydew melon

2 cups bite-size chunks ripe cantaloupe

2 cups seedless grapes

2 cups bite-size chunks pineapple

2 jalapeño peppers, stemmed, seeded, and finely diced

1/2 cup red currant preserves

Combine all the ingredients for the compote in a large bowl. Cover and chill before serving.

Makes 8 cups

Remove the thick outer skin of the ham and stud the surface with the cloves. Combine the preserves, vinegar, and mustard and coat the ham. (Reserve any left-over glaze.) Let the ham stand at room temperature for 1 hour to marinate.

Prepare an indirect fire on a barbecue grill or smoker, add apple, oak, or cherry wood to fire. Place the ham on the grill and smoke for 2 to 3 hours at 225 degrees F. Baste 2 or 3 times while smoking.

Serves 10 to 12

Pork and Pineapple Kabobs with Fruity Barbecue Sauce

Fresh fruit pairs well with meats on the grill. Substitute apples, peaches, pears, or the seasonal fruit of your choice. Serve with a fruit studded pasta or grain salad like couscous with dried apricots or bulgur with Mandarin oranges.

1 pound pork tenderloin, cut into 2-inch cubes

1 fresh pineapple, peeled, cored, and cubed

1 cup fruit-based barbecue sauce

WOOD:

1 cup of water-soaked fruit wood chips

Marinate the pork in ½ cup of the barbecue sauce for 1 hour in the refrigerator. Using 4 metal skewers, alternately thread the pork and pineapple onto the skewers. Or use kabob baskets and place pork and pineapple alternately in baskets.

Prepare a hot fire. Brush pork and pineapple with the remaining barbecue sauce. Add the wood chips to the hot fire, then cook the kabobs for about 10 to 15 minutes, turning frequently.

Serves 4

Hickory-Grilled Pork Burgers

Janeyce Michel-Cupito is an award-winning barbecue competitor and a fellow Que Queen. She offers this tasty recipe. Serve it with all the condiments like lettuce, tomato, avocado, red onion, mayonnaise, mustard, barbecue sauce, and crusty grilled Kaiser rolls.

1 to 1½ pounds coarsely ground pork butt

½ cup spicy tomato barbecue sauce

¼ cup chopped pistachios

1 tablespoon chopped fresh parsley

1 clove garlic, minced

WOOD:

1 cup of water-soaked hickory chips

Combine all ingredients and shape into four patties about ½ inch thick. Wrap in plastic wrap and refrigerate for 30 minutes to allow them to firm up.

Prepare a hot fire and add the hickory chips. Grill pork burgers for about 5 minutes each side until charred on the outside and done on the inside.

Serves 4

Herbed Smoked Pork Tenderloin

Pork is a versatile meat on the grill or smoker and marries well with just about any kind of wood you choose.

2 pork tenderloins, 8 ounces each

3/4 cup Italian dressing

1 teaspoon Worcestershire sauce

WOOD:

A handful of water-soaked wood chips (mesquite, oak, hickory, cherry, or apple)

Place all ingredients in a sealable plastic bag; seal bag and place in refrigerator for at least 20 minutes up to overnight.

Prepare a hot fire and add wood chips of your choice to the fire. Remove pork from the marinating bag and grill over a medium-hot fire, turning and basting until just done, about 15 minutes total cooking time. (The pork will firm to the touch as it cooks.) Slice the pork at a diagonal in 3/4-inch-thick slices and serve.

Serves 6

Sausage, Corn, and New Potato Kabobs

This recipe comes from Prairie Home Cooking *author Judith Fertig. Serve extra condiments like sauerkraut, German mustard, and chopped red onion with this meal for a taste of the heartland.*

1 pound smoked sausage or bratwurst

1 (12-ounce) can beer

1 pound small new potatoes, parboiled with skins on

2 to 3 ears fresh corn cut into 3- to 4-inch cobbettes, or use frozen

1/4 cup spicy mustard

1/4 cup cider vinegar

4 sourdough buns

WOOD:

A handful of water-soaked wood chips (alder, oak, hickory, or apple)

Marinate the smoked sausage in the beer for up to 1 hour. At the same time, in a separate container, combine the new potatoes and corn with the mustard and vinegar and marinate for up to 1 hour.

Prepare a hot grill. Drain the sausage and the vegetables and thread onto long metal skewers. Grill over a hot fire for 5 minutes on each side, or until the potatoes and corn are done.

Serve sausage on warmed buns along with the grilled potatoes and corn.

Serves 4

Fire-Flamed Barbecue Chicken

Serve this zesty hot chicken with couscous and a kiwi fruit salsa.

1 (2- to 3-pound) whole chicken, split
Salt and pepper to taste
1/2 cup barbecue sauce
1/3 cup orange marmalade
1 teaspoon Worcestershire sauce
1 teaspoon prepared horseradish
1/2 teaspoon hot pepper sauce

WOOD:
A handful of water-soaked wood chips (mesquite, oak, hickory, or apple)

Prepare a hot fire in the grill. Combine barbecue sauce, marmalade, Worcestershire sauce, horseradish, and hot pepper sauce in a small bowl for basting.

Grill the chicken over the hot coals for about 10 to 15 minutes to sear and mark, basting with mixture several times. Then place chicken on the indirect side of the grill and add wood chips to the fire. Maintain a medium-hot fire and cover. Continue basting chicken every 8 to 10 minutes, until done. Cooking time is about 45 to 50 minutes and internal temperature should be 180 degrees F. Let chicken rest for about 10 minutes before cutting into pieces.

Serves 4 to 6

Rosemary-Garlic Smoked Chicken

This is a fool-proof recipe that produces a luscious and juicy bird. Serve this with oven-roasted potatoes and butternut squash wedges seasoned with olive oil and fresh rosemary.

2 whole chickens (2 to 3 pounds each),
    giblets and necks removed

2 tablespoons olive oil

2 tablespoons chopped rosemary

2 heads of fresh garlic

WOOD:

A handful of water-soaked grapevine
    wood chips

Rinse chickens thoroughly and pat dry. Brush 1 tablespoon olive oil on each chicken and rub with 1 tablespoon rosemary. Cut about 1/2 inch off the top of each head of garlic and place in the cavity of each chicken.

Prepare smoker and add grapevine wood chips. Maintain a 225 degree F temperature and smoke for 2 1/2 hours. Chicken is done when the leg joint moves easily and the internal temperature taken in the thickest part of the thigh is 180 degrees F. Serve hot.

Serves 4 to 6

Herb and Citrus Smoked Chicken

You can never have too much smoked chicken on hand. Add it to salads or chowders, blend it with cream cheese and chopped peppers for a dip, use it to top a pizza, or combine it with crisp bacon for a club sandwich for lunch.

2 whole chickens (2 to 3 pounds each), giblets
    and necks removed

2 lemons

2 limes

6 tablespoons Italian herb seasoning

Salt and pepper to taste

WOOD:

3 to 5 water-soaked wood chunks (oak or apple)

Rinse chickens thoroughly and pat dry. Sprinkle each with the juice of 1 lemon and 1 lime inside and out. Place the lemon and lime halves in the cavity of each chicken and sprinkle 1 tablespoon of the herb seasoning inside each. Rub 2 tablespoons of the seasoning on the outside of each bird. Salt and pepper to taste.

Prepare the smoke for an indirect charcoal fire. Top with water-soaked hickory or apple wood chunks and smoke the chickens at 225 degrees F for about 3 to 4 hours. Chicken is done when the leg joint moves easily and the internal temperature is 180 degrees F. Serve hot.

Serves 4 to 6

Boardroom
Nuclear Chicken Wings

Courtesy of Que Queen Ann O'Meara's Boardroom Bar B-Q Restaurant. These wings go great with a frosty cold beer and a generous supply of napkins.

5 pounds chicken drummettes

1¹/2 cups barbecue spice

1 teaspoon ground red pepper

1 teaspoon black pepper or to taste

2 cups spicy tomato barbecue sauce

WOOD:

1¹/2 cups water-soaked wood chips (hickory
or mesquite)

Rinse the chicken well and drain. In a large paper or plastic bag, mix the spices and add the drummettes, several at a time. Close the bag and shake to dredge in the spice mixture. Let the chicken sit for an hour.

Prepare a hot indirect fire on the grill, adding wood chips (hickory and/or mesquite) as needed to provide a smokey flavor. Cook the chicken on the indirect side of the fire for 1 hour. Coat the drummettes with your favorite barbecue sauce and grill directly over the medium fire, turning constantly, until the drummettes are browned and done.

Makes about 60 wings to serve 10 to 12 as an appetizer

Fresh Herb Grilled Chicken

If you throw fresh snipped herbs onto your barbe-cue fire whenever you grill, it will scent the air as well as your food. Regular trimming is also good for coaxing more growth from your herb garden.

4 skinless, boneless chicken breasts

Olive oil

Freshly ground pepper

Assortment of fresh herb sprigs (parsley, sage, rosemary, and thyme)

 Rinse and dry chicken. Lightly brush olive oil on chicken and sprinkle generously with pepper.

Moisten herbs and place in an herb grill rack. Set rack over a medium-hot fire and place chicken atop rack. Grill for about 8 to 10 minutes, turning chicken halfway through grilling.

Serves 4

Dijon-Basted Chicken

This is a wonderfully easy and tasty entrée to serve with baked sweet potatoes, fresh asparagus or broccoli, and a crisp green salad.

8 boneless, skinless chicken breasts
1 cup Dijon mustard

WOOD:
1 cup water-soaked apple chips

Prepare a moderately hot fire in a charcoal or gas grill. Add the wood chips directly to the charcoal fire. Place the chips in a smoker box or in a loosely closed aluminum packet for the gas grill.

Brush the chicken breasts with the Dijon mustard and grill 2 minutes on each side to sear. Continue to baste with the sauce and turn until the chicken is browned on the outside and firm to the touch, about 8 minutes total.

Serves 6 to 8

Chicken Yakitori

According to the Food Lover's Companion, *yakitori is the Japanese term for "grilled" (yaki) "fowl" (tori), and usually refers to small pieces of skewered meat.*

2 boneless, skinless chicken breasts, cut into
    1-inch chunks

1/4 cup tomato-based barbecue sauce

1/4 cup sake or dry white wine

1 tablespoon vinegar

1 tablespoon soy sauce

1 teaspoon sugar

1 teaspoon grated fresh ginger

2 cloves garlic, minced

2 yellow or red bell peppers, seeded and cut
    into 1-inch squares

WOOD:

1 cup of water-soaked tea leaves or 6 bags
    of tea

Combine barbecue sauce, sake, vinegar, soy sauce, sugar, ginger, and garlic in a glass bowl. Add the chicken, cover, and marinate in the refrigerator for 2 hours. Remove chicken and discard the marinade. Thread chicken and peppers onto 4 metal skewers.

Prepare a hot fire and add the tea leaves to the fire. Grill over medium-high heat, turning often, for about 8 minutes, or until the chicken is cooked.

Serves 4

Shenandoah Valley Grilled Turkey Breast

For those who love turkey on the grill, this is a tangy recipe to add to your repertoire. Serve this with a vinegar coleslaw and a crusty round of artisan focaccia.

1 whole turkey breast, split
Salt and pepper to taste

WOOD:
A handful of water-soaked hickory chips

SHENANDOAH VALLEY VINEGAR BASTE:
1/2 cup vinegar
1/3 cup peanut oil
1/2 tablespoon poultry seasoning
1/2 tablespoon black pepper
2 teaspoons salt
1 teaspoon garlic powder
1 teaspoon hot sauce
1 teaspoon lemon juice

Rinse turkey breast and season with salt and pepper to taste. Combine all marinade ingredients in a bowl and whisk to blend.

Prepare a hot fire and add a handful of water-soaked hickory chips. Grill turkey over medium-hot fire for about 20 minutes, turning every 5 minutes. Continue grilling for another 20 to 25 minutes applying marinade liberally to turkey, while continuing to turn often. Turkey is done when it registers 170 to 175 degrees F on a meat thermometer inserted into the thickest part of the turkey.

Serves 6 to 8

Apple Smoked Turkey with Cranberry-Orange Salsa

Once you see how simple it is to smoke a turkey and how tasty the fragrant juicy meat is, you'll be hooked on smoking.

1 (10- to 13-pound) turkey
1 cup balsamic vinegar
1/4 cup water
3 tablespoons paprika
2 tablespoons sea salt
2 tablespoons lemon pepper
1/4 teaspoon marjoram

WOOD:
3 to 5 water-soaked apple wood chunks

CRANBERRY-ORANGE SALSA:
2 navel oranges
2 1/2 cups fresh cranberries
1 jalapeño pepper, stemmed, seeded, and diced
3/4 cup sugar

Zest the oranges and set aside. Peel and discard the remaining white membrane from the oranges. Chop the oranges and set aside. Rinse and sort the cranberries and chop coarsely in a food processor. Pour mixture into a bowl and add oranges, zest, jalapeño, and sugar and toss.

Makes about 2 cups

Place the well-rinsed turkey in an extra large sealable plastic bag.

Combine the vinegar, water, paprika, sea salt, lemon pepper, and marjoram in a glass jar and shake to blend. Add the marinade to the bag and marinate overnight in the refrigerator.

Remove turkey from refrigerator and set aside to come to room temperature, for about 1 hour. Build an indirect fire in a kettle grill or water smoker and add 3 apple wood chunks to the smoker. Remove the turkey from the marinade and place in the smoker. Smoke for 4 to 5 hours at

BARBECUE

225 degrees F until a meat thermometer inserted in the thickest part of the turkey thigh registers 170 degrees F. Halfway through the cooking time, add extra wood if necessary. Smoked turkey meat is a pale pink color.

Serves about 8

Lemon-Ginger Pork Chops

Grilled pork chops should be succulent and juicy, so don't overcook them! Serve them with a medley of grains or wild rice and a fresh seasonal vegetable.

4 (6-ounce) boneless pork chops

2 tablespoons lemon juice

2 tablespoons soy sauce

1 teaspoon grated fresh ginger

WOOD:

A handful of water-soaked wood chips (mesquite, oak, hickory, or apple)

Combine all ingredients, including the pork, in a sealable plastic bag and marinate in the refrigerator for up to 1 hour.

Prepare a hot fire in the grill and add a handful of your favorite wood chips to the fire. Grill chops over medium-hot fire for 5 to 6 minutes on each side.

Serves 4

Balsamic Grilled Swordfish

Feast on fresh grilled fish accompanied by sourdough baguettes with herb butter and a salad of mixed field greens.

4 large (1¼-inch-thick) swordfish steaks
    (may substitute salmon or tuna)
⅓ cup balsamic vinegar
⅓ cup olive oil
Salt and pepper to taste

WOOD:
A handful of water-soaked wood chips
    (alder or grape)

Rinse fish and pat dry, then place in a sealable plastic bag. Combine the vinegar and olive oil and pour $1/3$ cup over the fish. Reserve the remaining $1/3$ cup of vinegar and oil for basting. Seal the bag and marinate the fish in this mixture for 30 minutes in the refrigerator.

Prepare a hot fire and toss a handful of water-soaked wood chips onto the fire. Drain the fish and discard the marinade. Grill the swordfish over the hot fire for 5 to 6 minutes per side, basting several times with the reserved vinegar and oil. The fish is done when it feels firm to the touch and looks opaque. Season with salt and pepper to taste.

Serves 4

Tarragon-Infused Smoked Salmon

This versatile salmon recipe can be served as a main dish or it can be chilled to make a cold salmon salad or mixed with pasta to make a smoked salmon fettuccini Alfredo. As an appetizer, serve it with capers, chopped red onion, cream cheese, and lavosh crackers.

4 salmon steaks, 1 inch thick

1/2 cup Dijon mustard

2 tablespoons white wine vinegar

1/4 teaspoon red pepper flakes

8 to 10 sprigs fresh tarragon

WOOD:

3 or 4 chunks of water-soaked oak wood

Rinse the salmon steaks in cold water and pat dry with paper towels.

In a small bowl combine the mustard, vinegar, and pepper flakes. Marinate the salmon in the mixture for about 30 minutes. Place the fresh sprigs of tarragon in the bottom of a glass baking dish. Place the salmon on top of the tarragon.

Prepare a water smoker and add water-soaked oak chunks to the fire. Place the dish of salmon on the smoker rack. Smoke for about 1 hour or until salmon begins to flake when touched with a fork.

Serves 4

Fillet of Halibut with Grilled Red Onion Slices

Fish cooks very quickly and can fall apart on the grill if it is over-handled. For the best results, use a fish grilling rack or generously brush vegetable oil on your regular grill grate and grill fish for 10 minutes per inch of thickness, turning only once, halfway through the cooking.

1 halibut fillet, with skin intact (may substitute catfish)

1 red onion, sliced thick

A handful of fresh assorted herbs (optional)

TERIYAKI MARINADE:

1/4 cup teriyaki sauce

2 tablespoons vinegar

4 cloves garlic, minced

1 teaspoon dried ginger

1 teaspoon sesame oil

Place the fish fillet and onion slices in a nonreactive glass or stainless steel bowl or pan. Combine the marinade ingredients in a glass bowl, then pour over the fish and onion slices. Marinate for 15 to 30 minutes.

Prepare a hot fire and toss a handful of fresh herbs on the fire. Remove the halibut and onion slices from the marinade and place on a greased grill rack. Place fillet flesh side down on grill rack over hot coals. Grill fish for 10 minutes per inch of thickness, turning fish once, halfway through cooking time.

Serves 4

Two Martini Smoked Salmon

If you're a martini drinker, then you'll have most of these ingredients on hand. Leftover salmon combined with cream cheese and a little lemon juice makes a delicious paté appetizer to serve with a martini cocktail!

1 (3- to 4-pound) salmon, cleaned and scaled

1 lemon, sliced

6 fresh dill sprigs

1/4 cup gin or vodka

1/4 cup dry vermouth

1/4 cup fresh lemon juice

3 tablespoons butter, melted

1 tablespoon prepared horseradish

1/2 teaspoon hot sauce

1 clove garlic, minced

WOOD:

3 to 4 water-soaked chunks of alder or
    hickory wood

Prepare an indirect fire of water-soaked alder or hickory wood over charcoal.

Rinse the salmon and pat dry with paper towels. Place lemon slices and sprigs of dill in the cavity of the salmon. Set aside. Put the rest of the ingredients in a saucepan and bring to a boil, then set aside. Place the salmon on top of a piece of heavy-duty foil large enough to enclose the salmon. Crimp 3 sides to hold the baste (the other side will fold over). Pour the baste over the salmon, fold over the foil to enclose the salmon and crimp the edges together.

Place the salmon over a drip pan and smoke at 225 degrees F for 1 hour. Open the foil, but make sure edges stay crimped to hold in the baste. Smoke for 1 more hour, or until the fish flakes easily with a fork.

Serves 4 to 6

SMOKED TROUT GRAND MARNIER

For a beautiful presentation, thinly slice some extra lemons and limes and alternate them in a circular pattern on a platter. Place smoked trout on top of lemons and limes and serve.

4 whole rainbow trout, cleaned and scaled

1 lemon, sliced

1 lime, sliced

Salt and freshly ground pepper to taste

WOOD:

A handful of water-soaked wood chips (alder, pecan, oak, or mesquite)

GRAND MARNIER BASTE:

Juice of 1 lemon

Juice of 1 lime

3 tablespoons Grand Marnier

Combine basting ingredients and set aside. Rinse trout and pat dry. Place lemon and lime slices in cavity of each fish and season with salt and pepper.

Prepare a hot fire and add water-soaked wood chips for smoke. Grill trout over hot fire (use aluminum foil or a greased grill rack to keep fish from falling through grill grates). Brush with baste several times while grilling, about 6 to 7 minutes per side, or until fish begins to flake when pierced with a fork.

Serves 4

Smokey Grilled Shrimp Quesadillas

Smoked shrimp are so versatile—you can toss them into a salad, serve over some Spanish-style rice, pilaf, or pasta, or serve on toast for a fancy but easy hors d'oeuvre. Try these quesadillas for a cozy lunch or cut into slices as hot appetizers.

2 pounds large shrimp, peeled and deveined

1/2 cup Italian salad dressing

1/4 cup spicy barbecue sauce

4 flour tortillas

2 cups chopped scallions

1 cup grated Monterey jack cheese

1 cup grated queso (Mexican cheese) or
   cheddar cheese

WOOD:

1 cup water-soaked fruit wood chips

 In a bowl, combine the shrimp, Italian dressing, and barbecue sauce and set aside to marinate for 30 minutes. Place shrimp in a grill wok and drain over the kitchen sink. Place wok in a pan and carry out to the grill.

Prepare a hot fire and add water-soaked wood chips. Grill shrimp over a hot fire for about 7 to 8 minutes, tossing and basting with extra Italian dressing.

Preheat the oven to 350 degrees F. Place a few shrimp on a flour tortilla and top with $1/2$ cup of the chopped scallions and $1/2$ cup of the grated cheeses. Fold the sides of the tortillas into a triangle shape, top with more cheese, and place on a baking sheet. Repeat with the rest of the tortillas. Bake in the oven until the cheese melts. Remove from the oven and serve with sour cream and your favorite salsa.

Serves 4

Venison Chops with Cognac Mustard Sauce

Venison is a very lean meat and is best when prepared medium-rare.

4 venison or elk chops
Olive oil
Cracked pepper

WOOD:
1 cup water-soaked grapevines or wood chips

COGNAC MUSTARD SAUCE:
1/4 cup cognac
1/4 cup chicken stock
1/4 cup half and half
2 tablespoons Dijon mustard

Coat chops with oil and sprinkle with cracked pepper. Whisk all of the sauce ingredients together. Divide the sauce into two small bowls, refrigerating one bowl and using the other bowl for basting. (This avoids cross-contamination of the raw meat. You may use the refrigerated bowl as a serving sauce on the table.)

Prepare a hot fire and add grape wood. Grill chops over medium-hot fire for 3 to 4 minutes each side, basting several times with the sauce. Place the meat on the plates and serve with the extra bowl of sauce.

Serves 2

SMOKED STUFFED LEG OF LAMB À LA GRECQUE

As at home on a wine country terrace as it is in a wheat country backyard, this dish is perfect when the weather is cool. Make a double recipe of the Spinach Pesto and serve as an appetizer with bruschetta.

1 (6- to 7-pound) leg of lamb, boned, trimmed, and butterflied

WOOD:

5 water-soaked chunks of wood (apple, grape, peach, or oak)

SPINACH PESTO:

1 pound baby spinach leaves, rinsed, dried, and chopped

3 tablespoons olive oil

2 large cloves garlic, minced

1/2 cup fresh bread crumbs

1/4 cup chopped cured olives

¼ cup fresh chopped basil

1 (4-ounce) package feta cheese

½ teaspoon salt

¼ teaspoon ground pepper

In a medium skillet, heat the olive oil over high heat. Stir in the spinach and garlic, tossing and stirring often. Cook for 2 minutes or until the moisture has evaporated. Spoon the spinach mixture into a medium bowl and stir in the bread crumbs, olives, basil, feta cheese, salt, and pepper. Lay out the butterflied lamb and spread with the spinach mixture. Roll up lengthwise, jelly-roll style, and tie with twine at 1-inch intervals.

Prepare a smoker and add the wood. Smoke at 225 degrees F over an indirect fire for 4 to 5 hours, or until a meat thermometer inserted into the thickest part of the lamb registers at least 160 degrees F for medium.

Serves 6 to 8

Fresh Mint Basted Lamb Chops

Fresh herb basting brushes are fun to make. Use herbs with woody stalks like basil, mint, sage, lemon balm, rosemary, etc. Tie them together with twine or florist wire, then dip them in basting liquid and apply to items on the grill.

8 lamb chops, 3/4 inch thick

Salt and freshly ground pepper to taste

12 sprigs of fresh mint, 6 to 8 inches long

1/4 cup extra virgin olive oil

WOOD:

1 cup water-soaked wood chips (apple, mesquite, or grape)

Season the lamb chops with salt and pepper and set aside. Bundle the mint together with florist wire to make an herbal basting brush.

Prepare a hot fire and add the water-soaked wood chips. Place the chops over the medium-hot fire. Grill for about 7 minutes each side for a medium chop, basting with the mint brush and olive oil.

Serves 4 people 2 chops each

GRILLED WILD DUCK BREASTS

Duck is delicious served with a spoonful of tangy preserves like red currant, lingonberry, orange marmalade, or chutney.

4 wild duck breasts, cut in half

WOOD:
1 cup water-soaked wood chips (pecan shells, apple, oak, or cherry)

WATERFOWL MARINADE:
1 cup oil
1 cup white vinegar
1 teaspoon dried thyme leaves
1 teaspoon cayenne pepper
1 teaspoon dried basil
1 tablespoon black pepper
1 tablespoon garlic powder

Rinse duck breasts and place in a sealable plastic bag. Combine marinade ingredients in a glass bowl and add marinade to the plastic bag with the duck breasts. Seal and refrigerate overnight.

Prepare a hot fire and add wood chips. Grill over medium-hot fire for 5 to 8 minutes per side. Slice and fan breast meat for presentation.

Serves 4

Bacon-Wrapped Smoked Quail and Pheasant

This is a great two-dinner cook-out: Serve the quail dinner for four on the evening that you prepare it and save the pheasant for the next night's dinner!

8 quail, skinned and cleaned

1 pheasant, skinned, cleaned, and cut in half

10 slices of bacon (optional)

MARSALA MARINADE:

1/2 cup soy sauce

1/4 cup olive oil

1/4 cup Marsala wine

Zest and juice of 1 orange

2 cloves garlic, minced

Combine marinade ingredients and marinate quail and pheasant in the refrigerator overnight.

Remove from marinade and wrap each quail and pheasant half with 1 slice of bacon.

Prepare a grill for indirect cooking. Over the hot fire, sear pheasant for about 3 minutes per side and quail for about 2 minutes per side. Move pheasant bone-side down to the indirect side of grill. Stack quails on top of the pheasant. Cover grill with the lid and cook for 30 to 45 minutes. Game birds are done when the leg joints move easily. (Wild pheasant legs may be very tough depending on the age of the bird, and thus may be inedible.) Remove from the grill and serve immediately with wild rice and some sautéed vegetables.

Serves 8

Smokey Spicy Acorn Squash

Squash is a great winter vegetable. To create a one-pot dinner, prepare the squash and smoke it with turkey or chicken at the same time.

3 acorn squash, cut in half and seeded

3 teaspoons vegetable oil

6 tablespoons butter

2 teaspoons cinnamon

¼ cup brown sugar

½ teaspoon chili powder

WOOD:

3 water-soaked apple wood chunks

Brush the cut side of each squash half with the oil and cover each squash half with foil. Poke holes in the foil to let the smoke through.

Prepare a water smoker and add the apple wood chunks. Place squash cut-side down on a smoker rack. Smoke for 2 hours over indirect heat at 225 degrees F, or until the squash is tender. Remove from the smoker. Melt the butter in a small skillet and whisk in the rest of the ingredients. To serve, drizzle the spicy butter over the squash and serve.

Serves 6

Smoked Corn in the Husk

Smoke extra corn for use in soups and salads, or make a smoked corn relish with chopped onion, peppers, and a vinaigrette dressing.

6 to 12 ears of fresh corn, in the husk

1/2 cup olive oil

1 bunch of green onions, finely chopped

WOOD:

3 chunks of water-soaked wood (oak, apple, peach, or mesquite)

Pull back the husks from each ear and remove the corn silk. Pull the husks back over the corn and set them in a large pan. Cover the corn with water and let soak for several hours. Drain. Partially pull back husks again and brush each ear with olive oil, then add 1 to 2 teaspoons of chopped green onion. Close up the husks.

Prepare a smoker and smoke with wood of your choice over indirect heat at 225 degrees F for $1^1/_2$ hours, or until the corn is tender. Pull the husks back and use as a handle to enjoy your delicious corn.

Serves 6 to 8

Smokey Horseradish Potatoes

Try substituting sweet potatoes or turnips for the russet potatoes in this recipe.

8 large russet potatoes, peeled and roughly
    chopped

1 cup heavy cream

4 tablespoons butter

1 tablespoon horseradish, or to taste

Salt and pepper to taste

WOOD:

3 chunks of water-soaked wood (apple, hickory,
    maple, or oak)

Put the potatoes in a large pot and cover with water. Bring to a boil and cook for 15 minutes, or until the potatoes are soft. Drain the water and mash with the cream and butter until smooth. Blend in the horseradish and season to taste. Place mixture in a casserole dish.

Prepare smoker by adding wood to the unit. Place potato casserole in smoker and smoke at 225 degrees F for 1 hour.

Serves 8

SMOKED BAKED POTATOES WITH CAVIAR SOUR CREAM

*Make these potatoes a main course meal by serving
with an assortment of toppings such as bacon bits,
avocado, chopped smoked meats, chopped
scallions, parsley, chives, cilantro, and salsa.*

8 to 10 potatoes
Vegetable oil
Garlic salt

WOOD:
3 or 4 chunks of water-soaked oak, mesquite, or
   hickory

CAVIAR SOUR CREAM:
1/2 cup sour cream
2 tablespoons lemon juice
2 tablespoons salmon caviar

Combine sour cream and lemon juice, then gently stir in the caviar. Chill in the refrigerator before serving.

Makes about 3/4 cup

Scrub the potatoes and prick with a fork. Rub with vegetable oil and sprinkle with garlic salt.

Prepare smoker by adding the wood and smoke over indirect heat for 2 hours at 225 degrees F or until the potatoes are done. To serve, split the potatoes and top with Caviar Sour Cream.

Serves 8 to 10

Smoked Stuffed Mushrooms

If you're planning an outdoor barbecue, this appetizer will get your party off to a great start.

24 large mushrooms, cleaned
2 tablespoons vegetable oil
1 medium onion, peeled and chopped
8 ounces cream cheese, softened
1/2 cup mozzarella cheese, shredded
2 teaspoons Italian seasoning
Salt and pepper to taste
2 tablespoons chopped fresh parsley

Assorted fresh herbs to throw on the fire

Stem the mushrooms and chop the stems finely. Heat the oil in a skillet and sauté the stems with the onion for about 5 minutes, then set aside. In a food processor, blend the cream cheese, mozzarella, Italian seasoning, salt, and pepper. Transfer to a bowl and blend in the parsley and onion mixture. Stuff the mushrooms.

Prepare the grill or a smoker and add the fresh herbs to the fire (or put herbs loosely in foil and place on a gas grill). Arrange the mushrooms on a baking sheet and smoke using the indirect method at 225 degrees F for 1 hour.

Serves 8

Smoked Vegetables with Lemon-Rosemary Vinaigrette

Rosemary is one of the most fragrant herbs. It always reminds me of Provence and the Mediterranean. Serve these vegetables over rice with a dry white wine like Pinot Grigio or a Provencal rosé.

4 Vidalia, or other variety of sweet onions, peeled and cut in sixths

6 tomatoes, cored and cut in quarters

2 yellow bell peppers, cored, seeded, and cut in sixths

2 red bell peppers, cored, seeded, and cut in sixths

WOOD:

3 or 4 chunks of water-soaked apple and mesquite

LEMON-ROSEMARY VINAIGRETTE:

1/4 cup chopped fresh rosemary leaves (2 tablespoons dry)

1/2 cup olive oil

1/4 cup fresh lemon juice

Salt and pepper to taste

Whisk together the rosemary, olive oil, lemon juice, and seasonings in a small bowl. Using a small knife, mark the surface of each vegetable, then place vegetables in a nonreactive pan or bowl. Pour the marinade over the vegetables, toss to coat, and set aside to marinate for at least 30 minutes. Drain the vegetables, reserving the marinade, and arrange them in a disposable aluminum pan.

Prepare a smoker by adding the apple and mesquite wood chunks. Smoke the vegetables at 250 degrees F for 30 minutes to an hour, basting frequently with the vinaigrette, until the vegetables are soft. Arrange on a platter and serve.

Serves 6

SMOKEY SPICY ASSORTED NUTS

Nuts on the smoker are delicious and so easy to do. Make a double batch and give some as a gift to a friend or neighbor.

3 teaspoons curry powder

1/4 cup Worcestershire sauce

1/2 cup water

2 teaspoons sugar

2 garlic cloves, minced

1 teaspoon salt

2 cups pecans

1 cup peanuts

1 cup cashews

WOOD:

3 to 4 water-soaked chunks of wood (hickory or mesquite)

 Combine curry powder, Worcestershire sauce, water, sugar, garlic, and salt in a bowl. Add nuts and marinate for an hour. Drain and spread the nuts out in a disposable aluminum pan.

Prepare a smoker by adding the wood. Smoke at 225 degrees F for 1 hour, or until the nuts are crisp and lightly smoked. Serve immediately or keep in an airtight container.

Makes 3 cups

Holiday Smoked Pizza

During the holidays, there's usually an abundant supply of leftover smoked ham or turkey. Try this pizza as a festive hors d'oeuvre or a quick supper.

1 large Boboli or a previously baked pizza shell

8 ounces cream cheese, softened

1/2 cup country-style Dijon mustard

1/2 pound barbecued smoked ham or turkey

1/2 cup chutney

 Prepare a hot grill or preheat the oven to 400 degrees F. Place the pizza shell on a large baking sheet. Spread cream cheese over the pizza crust, then spread the mustard on top of the cream cheese. Arrange the smoked meat on top and spoon dollops of the chutney around the pizza. Grill indirectly for about 15 minutes or until the cream cheese has melted. Cut into wedges and serve piping hot.

Serves 4

Books on Barbecue

The popularity of cookbooks available for grilling and smoking enthusiasts is ever growing. Here is a list of favorites, some old and some new. For a complete list of titles on outdoor cooking visit the following website: www.pigoutpublications.com.

Barbecue America by Rick Browne and Jack Bettridge
    (1999, Time Life Books)
Barbecue Greats Memphis Style by Carolyn Wells
    (1992, Pig Out Publications)
Barbecued Ribs by Karen Adler (2000, Pig Out Publications)
Barbecuing and Sausage-Making Secrets by Charlie and Ruthie Knote
    (1993, Culinary Institute of Smoke Cooking)
Cooking with Fire and Smoke by Phillip Stephen Schulz
    (1986, Simon & Schuster)
Great American BBQ & Grill Manual by Smoky Hale
    (2000, Abacus Publishing)
Great Ribs Book by Hugh Carpenter and Teri Sandison
    (1999, Ten Speed Press)
Kansas City Barbeque Society Cookbook
    (1996, Kansas City Barbeque Society)
Que Queens–Easy Grilling & Simple Smoking by Karen Adler &
    Judith Fertig (1997, Pig Out Publications)
Smoke & Spice by Cheryl and Bill Jamison (1994, Harvard Common Press)
Sublime Smoke by Cheryl and Bill Jamison (1996, Harvard Common Press)
Where There's Smoke There's Flavor by Richard W. Langer
    (1996, Little, Brown and Company)
Wild About Kansas City Barbecue by Rich Davis and Shifra Stein
    (2000, Pig Out Publications)
Wild About Texas Barbecue by John Bigey and Paris Permenter
    (2000, Pig Out Publications)

CONVERSIONS

LIQUID
1 tablespoon = 15 milliliters
1/2 cup = 4 fluid ounces = 125 milliliters
1 cup = 8 fluid ounces = 250 milliliters

DRY
1/4 cup = 4 tablespoons = 2 ounces = 60 grams
1 cup = 1/2 pound = 8 ounces = 250 grams

FLOUR
1/2 cup = 60 grams
1 cup = 4 ounces = 125 grams

TEMPERATURE
400 degrees F = 200 degrees C = gas mark 6
375 degrees F = 190 degrees C = gas mark 5
350 degrees F = 175 degrees C = gas mark 4

MISCELLANEOUS
2 tablespoons butter = 1 ounce = 30 grams
1 inch = 2.5 centimeters
all purpose flour = plain flour
baking soda = bicarbonate of soda
brown sugar= demerara sugar
confectioners' sugar = icing sugar
heavy cream = double cream
molasses= black treacle
raisins = sultanas
rolled oats = oat flakes
semisweet chocolate = plain chocolate
sugar= caster sugar